Sharks and Whales

by Burton Albert

Illustrated by Pamela Baldwin Ford

Platt & Munk, Publishers/New York
A Division of Grosset & Dunlap

1980 PRINTING

Great White Shark. *A loner. Man-eater. The white death. The most dangerous creature alive.* That's the great white shark, with its unblinking black eyes and row after row of 50 sawlike teeth, each two-inches long. But the teeth are not used for chewing. They are used for crushing and tearing, since this shark swallows its food whole.

In one instance, a shark swallowed the body of a horse heaved from a garbage barge. A great white also gouged an eight-inch hole in a rowboat. Another left its entire jaw locked in the hull of a clipper ship. The great white, you see, stops at nothing!

Angel Shark. As sharks evolved over millions of years, they divided into two groups. The larger group became the cigar-shaped sharks. The other turned into flat-bodied skates and rays. With winglike fins, skates and rays "fly" through the water.

Today's rare angel shark looks like a ray. It grows to four or five feet—about as long as your outstretched arms. When seen, it is often close to shore, partly buried in the sand.

Port Jackson Shark. Unlike most sharks, the Port Jackson has two kinds of teeth. With pointed teeth near the front of its mouth, it picks up shellfish to eat. Then it crushes the shells with rear teeth that are flat.

Among its 250 or so "relatives," the Port Jackson looks most like the first kind of shark that ever lived.

Nurse Shark. With long whiskers drooping from its nostrils, the nurse doesn't look like a shark. And unlike most sharks that need to keep moving in order to breathe, the lazy nurse can pump water through its gill slits while lying still, often resting its head under a shallow, sea-bottom ledge. The nurse shark, which preys on spiny lobsters, is itself a tempting target for skindivers who mistake it for a porpoise. They grab hold of its tail for a free ride . . . and a most startling surprise — a bite from a grumpy ''nurse''!

Blue Shark. More ''great blues'' roam the ocean than any other large sharks. Slimly built, a blue can sprint up to 45 miles per hour and cruise for many miles at half that speed. But it rarely nears the shallows. Instead, it travels offshore in packs of hundreds and even thousands. It feeds on herring, mackerel, other fish, birds, and dead whales. Many people believe that blue sharks have also devoured victims of downed planes and disabled ships.

Basking Shark. "Helm alee! A monster . . . a sea serpent!" sailors once shouted. And that's exactly what five or six basking sharks look like when they swim nose to tail, nose to tail. This habit has also won them the name elephant shark, a name that fits their size as well. They love to cruise on the sunny surfaces of the water. There they sift tons of tiny sea life, called krill, through the gill rakers that stretch across their throats.

Lemon Shark. This dangerous, sharp-eyed shark prefers saltwater creeks and bays. There it probably feeds on skates, rays, and small fish. It has also attacked swimmers.

When any shark breaks a tooth, a back-up tooth takes its place. But a young lemon shark loses so many teeth, it replaces whole sets of teeth every eight or ten days!

Dusky Shark. What a bite this shark has! When one of these eight-footers sinks its teeth into a dolphin, the strength of its press is enormous. Every square inch of where the teeth strike gets as much pressure as if three or four elephants were standing on it. So imagine the *hundreds* of elephants that must equal the power of the dusky's huge bite.

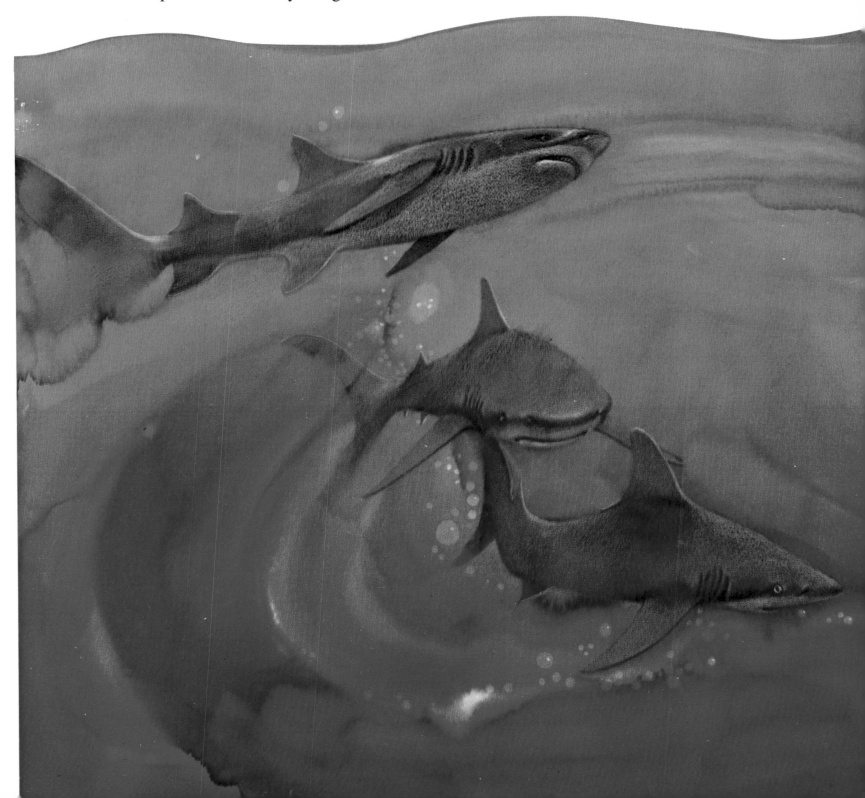

Thresher Shark. Because it has a small mouth and small teeth, the thresher doesn't depend on its teeth. It uses its long, sickle-shaped tail to thrash the water and round up schools of herring or the like. Then the shark rams the frantic fish, stuns a mass of them, releases the rest, and devours the dazed. At times it can toss a fish into its mouth with the simple flick of the tail that gives the thresher its nickname—sea fox.

Large and Small Black-Tipped Sharks. They're acrobats. When hooked, they leap and spin in midair, a breath-taking sight.

The small black-tipped shark has bigger eyes than its cousin, but both can see and smell the shrimp boats they trail. Schools pierce the nets or feed on the trash fish shoveled overboard. During a bloody feast, the frenzied sharks churn the waters into foam.

Bull Shark. This slow-moving shark feeds close to shore. It also travels up rivers. Pilot fish glide along its side. Some experts say the bull shark kills more people than does any other kind of sea creature.

Many bull sharks live in a large freshwater lake in Central America. Fifteen miles away, in another lake, there are no sharks. Both lakes, however, are connected by a river. So why does one body of water have sharks, and the other, none? It's still a puzzle.

Great Hammerhead. Old UglyPuss won't win any beauty contests. Just look at that face and head! It's five times wider than the rest of the shark's body. Even the eyes are set three feet apart. So, too, are the nostrils. Yet this distance seems perfect for protecting the shark from the dangerous and painful tail-whip of a stingray, the hammerhead's favorite meal.

Greenland Shark. Among sharks, the Greenland rules the Arctic waters. It spends all of its life there and feeds on squid, salmon, and seals. It is sometimes called a "sleeper" because it merely moseys about to save energy in the freezing cold.

Unless they have to, Eskimos will not eat a Greenland without preparing it carefully. Its flesh is slightly poisonous and can make a person feel drunk and sick. The Greenland's a real stinker, for it smells of ammonia as well.

Sleeping Shark. These sharks were found recently in some caves in Mexico. There, in fresh water, they lay motionless as if asleep.

A woman who studied this kind of shark believes that the fresh water loosens the barnacles and other tiny animals that grow on the shark's body. The remora, a fish that rides the shark, gives its host a ''cleaning'' by eating the loosened animals.

Dogfish. "What pests!" a fisherman will tell you. For these small sharks not only eat crabs but feast upon boating equipment, too.

There are 30 different kinds. Few grow beyond three feet—a yardstick long. Seldom does one weigh more than 10 pounds.

The female spiny dogfish carries her babies for two years before they are born. That's a record time for any animal with a spinal column. Another kind of dogfish gives off its own light. How it does this is known, but *why* it does is another mystery of the sea.

Mitsukurina. When Japanese fishermen caught this extremely rare fish off the coast of Yokahama, they called it "goblin shark." And a stranger, more prehistoric-looking creature never swam the seas. Mitsukurina has a long, dagger-shaped horn growing out of its forehead.

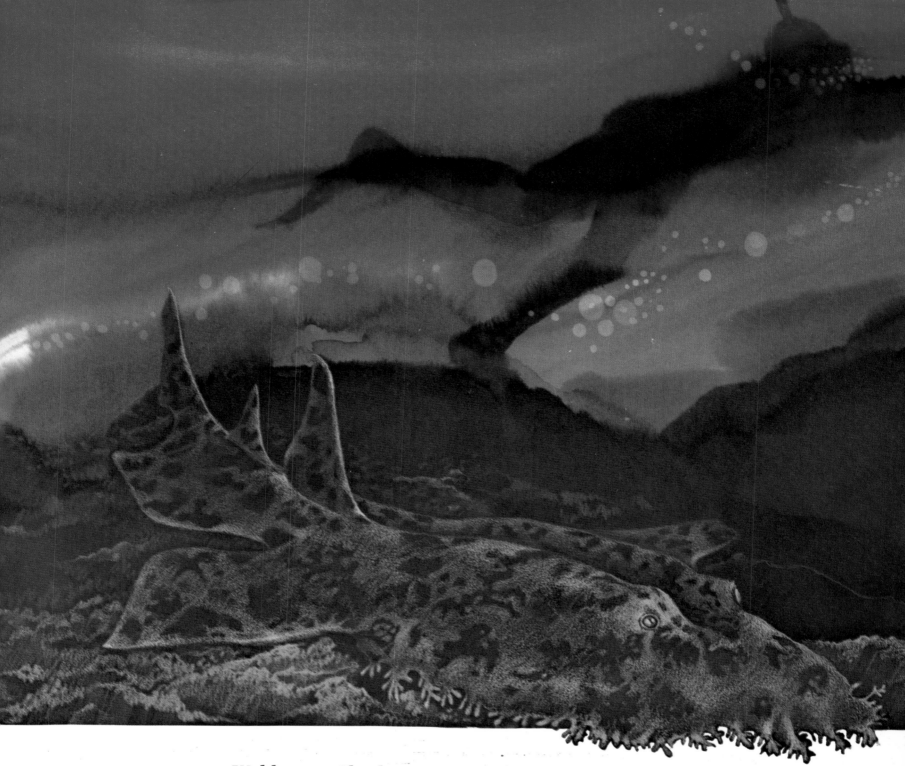

Wobbegong Shark. Look again—closely! Find the animal with the tassel-trimmed mouth.

Yes, it's hard to see the wooby, or carpet shark. Its marblelike markings match the floor of the sea, where it spends its day. Because a swimmer can't see the shark either, it is easy to step on.

A wooby's favorite food is crayfish. It will even invade a crayfish pot, or trap, to reach its ocean-bottom treat.

Swell Shark. The swell shark grows only as long as two or three of these books placed end-to-end. It likes to lurk in beds of seaweed. But if something disturbs this shark, it fills its body with air and floats on the surface.

Sand Tiger Shark. Sand tigers travel in schools, linger near beaches, and swallow food whole—such as eels or crabs. Like swell sharks, they can suck air into their stomachs and float.

Sand tigers are the only known creatures to have babies that kill each other before they are born. The strongest one hatched from thousands of eggs eats the other babies *inside* the mother's body.

Mako Shark. From cobalt blue above to snow-white below, the mako is a beautiful shark. It is also one of the fastest in the world. Just think how it must streak to catch its natural enemy, the broadbill swordfish. The fish itself pierces the water at speeds up to 60 miles an hour. That's faster than most cars zoom by on a thruway.

Usually, though, the mako feeds on schools of squid, herring, and bottom fish. When caught on hook and line, it whirls and spins and leaps as high as a cabin cruiser.

Porbeagle. "You'd better watch out or the bogeyman will get you." That's how a child today might threaten another child. In ancient Greece, children played the same game. But they gave their make-believe creature the name porbeagle, which meant "man-eating monster." The porbeagle shark is very swift and acts much like the mako but prefers colder waters. It follows and feeds on schools of mackerel.

Tiger Shark. This night prowler loses its tigerish brown stripes as it ages. It often trails fishing boats, tears into nets, and feasts upon the catch. During an attack, schools of tigers seem to go crazy. They even bite the boat's rudder and anchor.

A tiger shark will gobble anything—from a whole sea turtle to a 30-foot roll of roofing paper. In fact, one shark downed some canned goods, a leather wallet, a coil of wire, a sack of coal, a driver's license, and an 18-pound tom-tom. This creature is among the most feared of the man-eaters.

Whaler Shark. More than one hundred years ago, sailors on whaling ships in Australia named this shark. It would trail the wash of waves and rip away parts of the harpooned whales that the men were towing ashore. Today, in that part of the world, this 700-pounder rivals the tiger shark as the deadliest fish. Its victims include humans.

Whale Shark. The whale, or checkerboard, shark is the giant of the fish world. It is as long as a trailer truck and weighs as much as ten big horses. Its jaws can open wide enough to swallow humans. But, strange as it may seem, the whale shark feeds only on the smallest of sea life—shrimp, plankton, and baby fish.

Sometimes the whale shark ''stands'' straight up and puts its mouth just above the sea. Then it pumps up and down, up and down. As the water swirls and whirls and swishes, little fish are swept into the monster's mouth.

Sperm Whale. ''Thar she blows!'' bellowed sailors of old. They could tell by its forward-slanting spout that a great sperm whale was swimming up ahead. A huge mammal, it was hunted mainly for heating and lighting oil. Today these needs can be filled in other ways, so further killing of this whale is senseless.

The shape of the sperm is one that toy whales are often given. Its head measures about one-third the size of its body and contains a brain that is the largest of any animal on earth. The sperm can grow as long as 60 feet. The average male can weigh as much as 15 to 20 middle-sized cars. The sperm can also stay underwater for 90 minutes and dive deeper than any other whale. The sperm whale has 50 to 60 teeth, all in its lower jaw. They fit into openings in the upper jaw and they are used for attacking sharks, fish, octopus, and giant squid.

Greenland Right Whale. Some whales, like the sperm, have teeth. Others have *balleen,* which is also called whalebone and is made of the same material as your fingernails.

As a balleen whale skims the surface of the sea, it gulps a huge amount of water that blows up its throat and chest. Then the whale closes its mouth and squirts the water out through its balleen ''moustache.'' The balleen traps tiny sea animals upon which the whale feeds.

The Greenland has 700 of these balleen plates hanging from its upper jaw. Each has feathery edges and stands two brooms high.

Long ago, whalers named these creatures, which lived only in the Arctic. They were slow-moving, just ''right'' to catch. So easy was the kill that today hardly any of these great balleens are left.

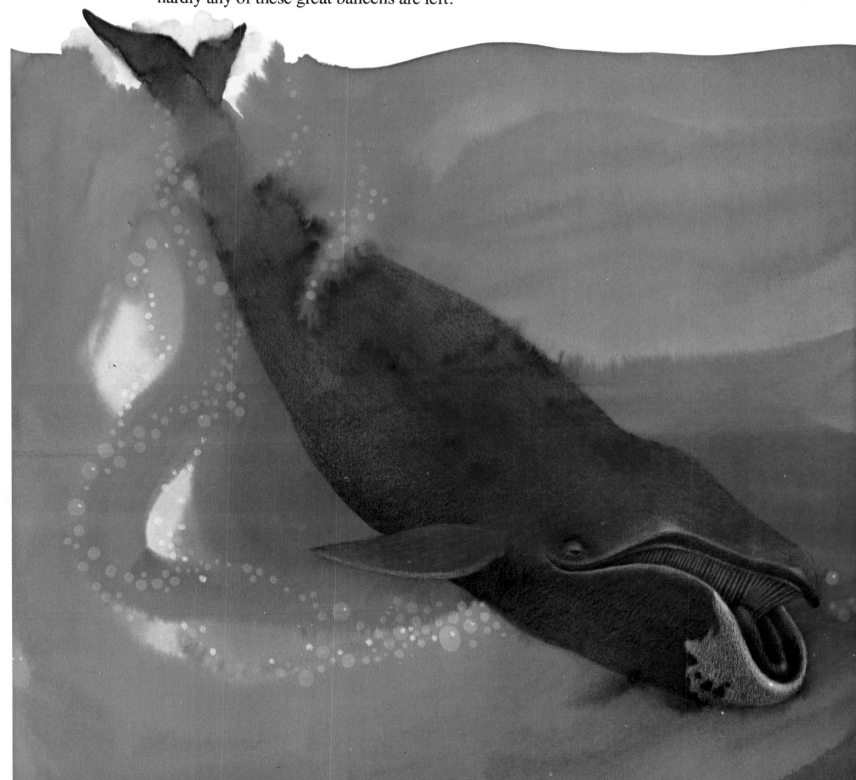

Black Right Whale. This big-headed hulk wears a bumpy bonnet. It's made of horny, rough skin and has creases filled with whale lice. Its cavelike mouth has 500 or more balleen plates.

Black rights usually travel in twos. They prefer cool waters close to island clusters. Because of the large number that has been slaughtered—by groups of killer whales as well as by humans—the black right may be the rarest of all the great whales.

Pilot Whale. The pilot whale plays follow-the-leader. Wherever the biggest old male goes, so go thousands of others. They'll follow him blindly, even getting stranded ashore, where they whimper like babies and die.

This three-tonner is one of the very few all-black whales. With small, pointed teeth, it feeds mainly at night on squid, octopus, and the like. When it spouts, it also barks—a sound that people enjoy at water shows where pilot whales sometimes perform.

California Gray Whale. These hairy, cigar-shaped creatures put on their show at sea. People watch while schools of hundreds sail along the west coast to winter in the lagoons of Southern California. To get there, the whales travel 4000 to 6000 miles from the Arctic. Some scientists think the whales do not rest or eat during the three-month journey.

Sometimes, if a whale comes too close to shore, its weight can crush or smother it. Other times, the gray simply lies around and waits for the tide to rise and refloat it.

Humpback. What an athlete! Despite its size and weight—45 feet and 50 tons—the humpback rolls, leaps, swims on its back, and even turns complete somersaults in the water.

What a singer, too! It produces long, slow, complicated songs that last from six minutes to half an hour. To some listeners, the songs sound like the squeaks of a rusty hinge or an orchestra playing off key. To others, it's the sound of bagpipes and oboes—the most beautiful sound in the world. Yet the "beautiful music" may end if the killing of the humpback continues.

Killer Whale. Twelve, two-inch teeth in each jaw of the killer whale are set like this ![teeth] . So when the eight-ton creature attacks, its teeth interlock for gripping and tearing.

If the killer circles and closes in on a great whale, its teeth go first for the victim's tongue. Then the killer lets the victim bleed to death before chomping on the carcass. Killers also feast on porpoises, seals, sharks, penguins, squid, fish, and even dead whales being towed by factory ships. In an aquarium, however, the killer is gentle, probably because its handlers feed it well.

Common Dolphin. This member of the whale family usually performs in the bow waves of ships. There it leaps and frolics in schools of up to 200.

With 40 or 50 teeth in each jaw, the dolphin feeds on sardines, herring, squid, and crabs. And at times it taunts a sea turtle or a fish the way a cat plays with a mouse.

Dolphins show great affection among themselves. If one is sick or wounded, others will hold it above water with their heads—for days—so the sick dolphin can breathe as it gets well. Likewise, a mother dolphin becomes very concerned about her newborn. She will not let it wander more than ten feet away. At birth she may choose another female to become the baby's ''aunt.''

Bottlenosed Dolphin. One bottlenosed dolphin was the star of a television series. Others perform in water shows and movies. They are longer and fatter than common dolphins and have only half as many teeth. But like all dolphins, the bottlenosed makes use of echo location. That is, it gives off a number of different sounds—from those we cannot hear to those that sound like clicks. Vibrations from the sounds bounce back through the water and tell the dolphin the size and shape of any object in its path.

Risso's Dolphin. This friendly creature has a bulging forehead that makes it look like a pilot whale. It also is larger than most dolphins. Sometimes it grows as long as thirteen of these books.

The Risso has been known to make regular trips with boats. The most famous Risso was Pelorus Jack. He guided the ferry from Wellington to Nelson, New Zealand through a body of water called Pelorus Sound. He did this each day for 30 years!

Susu. In the muddy Ganges River of India where this small, five-foot dolphin lives, hardly anything can be seen. So the susu has nearly gone blind. It depends on its pointed snout to dig up dinner. A susu is named for the noise it makes as it breathes.

Amazon River Dolphin. With very tiny eyes, very big cheeks, and a very long snout, this South American whale cannot see downward. But its eyes can see upward. So this animal, which is not much larger than a susu, swims upside-down at the bottom of the river to get its food. Because of the color of its belly, it is also called the pink porpoise.

Chinese Lake Dolphin. Some people think this creature may be blind. It lives only in the Tung Ting Lake in China. With nearly 140 teeth, it feeds on fish, shrimp, crabs, and the like. Its dorsal, or rear, fin gives this strange whale its more common name—white flag dolphin.

Cross River Dolphin. Unlike the river dolphins that feed on mud-living fish, this African animal is the one member of the whale family that feeds only on vegetables. It eats mangrove leaves, water weeds, and grasses.

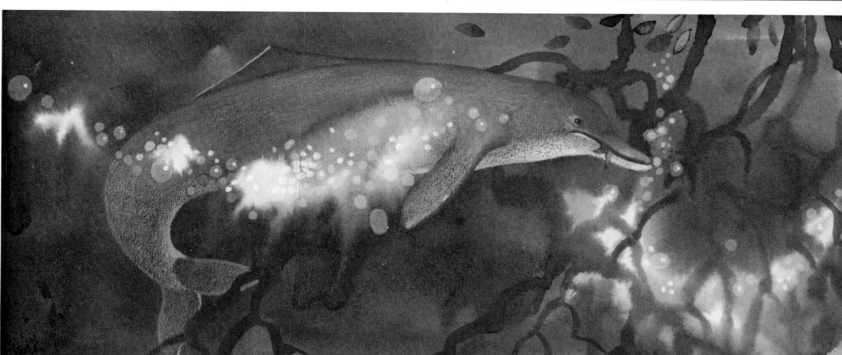

Common Porpoise. To tell a dolphin from a porpoise, look for a beak. The dolphin has one. The porpoise has none.

One of the smallest of all whales, the porpoise grows about as long and as heavy as a Great Dane or an Irish wolfhound. Although it acts like a dolphin, the porpoise likes to travel in small groups. It also prefers to linger near a coast.

Sounds from porpoises are many and varied. One sound is given off by the strongest porpoise in a group. The signal seems to mean, "Stay away from that fish, it's mine!"

Finback Whale. Longer than most houses and heavier than a dozen elephants, the finback is the second largest whale. Its two blowholes produce a spout as high as a giraffe. Sometimes this graceful mammoth leaps straight out of the water and splashes on its side in a thundering roar.

The finback, an endangered whale, is the only one with its odd coloring. Its lower left jaw is black. The lower right is white. Its 250 to 450 pairs of balleen plates are blue-gray on the left and pale yellow on the right. Each day they sift enough krill to equal 36,000 hamburgers.

Minke Whale. In the cold waters where it likes to spend its summers, the minke whale might be seen resting its head on an ice floe. In fact, this balleen goes closer to the South Pole than any other whale. It can grow as long as two vans and weigh as much as five middle-sized cars.

Alone or in small schools, it often follows ships and dives under them. This habit, however, is increasing the number of minke deaths. Some of the ships are on the prowl, ready to torpedo harpoons into the sides of these playful creatures.

Narwhal. The male narwhal has a tusk that looks like that of the unicorn, the mythical horse with a horn. But the tusk is really the upper left tooth grown to eight or nine feet. Some think the tusk is used for fighting or chipping air holes in the icy waters where the narwhal lives. Others think the twisted tooth may be used to dig food from the sea bottom, to spear fish, or to attract females. The pale gray coloring of the narwhal gives the 12- to 20-foot creature its name. It means "corpse whale."

Northern Bottlenosed Whale. This 10-ton creature can deep-dive for up to a half hour. It summers in the Arctic and winters in warmer waters. The bottlenosed has only one pair of teeth. They are in the lower jaw. Its mouth has a lining, however, that looks like pink terry cloth. This nubby texture helps the bottlenosed whale hold on to its favorite meal—the thrashing, slippery squid.

Beluga Whale. The only completely white whale is the beluga. It is a deep-diving creature that lives in the Arctic Ocean. It can swim under the ice and use breathing holes made by seals. With 36 to 40 teeth, it feeds on fish, squid, cuttlefish, and crabs. Although it may travel in groups of a dozen, at times it may roam with larger herds numbering 800 to 1000. The beluga is preyed upon by the killer whale. It also makes a hearty dinner for the polar bear.

Sei Whale. Each year in Norway the sei appears at the same time as the
seje, the pollack that gives the whale its name. Although it can grow as long as
three station wagons and weigh as much as six of them, the sei is a swift
swimmer. It can sprint at speeds of up to 35 miles an hour. And after a
10-minute dive, it can spout as high as a one-story house.

The sei feeds on krill, sardines, and the like. Its balleen has fringe as fine as
silk. Unfortunately, because so many blue and finback whales have been killed,
whalers in some countries are turning to the sei. Now its life is endangered.

Bryde's Whale. The Bryde's whale looks like the sei's twin. A close examination shows, however, that it is more streamlined than the sei and has three ridges on top of its head rather than one.

On each side of the Bryde's jaw are 250 to 290 balleen plates. They are short, wide, and thick. They sift sardine, mackerel, and shoalfish from the warm ocean waters where the Bryde likes to roam. Schools of 100 or more are an amazing sight!

Blue Whale. This is the largest animal ever to have lived. It grows as long as a railroad car and as wide as a two-story house. It weighs as much as 20 or 30 elephants. No wonder it uses more than 700 balleen plates to sift four tons of krill a day!

The whale's heart weighs as much as 20 six-year-old children. Blood vessels leading from the heart are tunnels as round as fire hydrants.

A baby blue is hefty. Each day it drinks half a ton of milk from its mother and puts on 220 pounds!

Until now, a blue whale has usually lived for 100 years. But if the killing of the blue goes on, there may be none left to live that long again.